THE TUILERIES GARDENS YESTERDAY AND TODAY
A WALKER'S GUIDE

AUTHOR

Emmanuelle Héran
Senior Curator, in charge of the Tuileries Garden Heritage

MUSÉE DU LOUVRE

Jean-Luc Martinez
President-Director
Karim Mouttalib
General Administrator
Valérie Forey-Jauregui
Assistant General Administrator

Mediation and Cultural Programming Department
Vincent Pomarède
Deputy Director
Aline François Colin and Michel Antonpietri
Assistants Deputy Director
Laurence Castany
Deputy Manager of Production and Publication Services

Architectural Heritage and Gardens Department
Sophie Lemonnier
Deputy Director
Isabelle Glais
Head of Gardens Division

PUBLICATION

Musée du Louvre, Publication Service
Violaine Bouvet-Lanselle
Head of Publication Service

Somogy Art Publishers
Nicolas Neumann
Director
Stéphanie Méséguer
Managing Editor
Pauline Desert, Chloé Fouquet and Léa Pietton
Iconography
Béatrice Bourgerie and Mélanie Le Gros
Technical Production

Pauline Garrone
Editorial Coordination
Carine Simon
Graphic Design
Thierry Renard
Cartographer
David and Jonathan Michaelson
Translation from French to English
Katharine Turvey
Editorial Contribution

© Somogy éditions d'art, Paris, 2016
www.somogy.fr
© musée du Louvre, Paris, 2016
www.louvre.fr

ISBN musée du Louvre: 978-2-35031-546-1
ISBN Somogy: 978-2-7572-1103-8
Dépôt légal: May 2016
Printed in Czech Republic (European Union)

jardin des Tuileries

EMMANUELLE HÉRAN

THE TUILERIES GARDENS

YESTERDAY AND TODAY

A Walker's Guide

SOMOGY ÉDITIONS D'ART

LOUVRE éditions

1. Claude Monet (1840–1926), *The Tuileries*, 1876, oil on canvas, Musée Marmottan Monet, Paris.

———————

This guide aims to highlight the rich past and contemporary diversity of the Tuileries Gardens, as these historical gardens were first created five centuries ago. They were initially intended as an area for recreation and leisure activities, and, although the gardens were reserved solely for members of the royal court for many years, they are now open to the general public. Some long-standing practices have disappeared, while others have survived and evolved. From the outset, the Tuileries have always been a melting pot of innovation for gardeners, landscape architects, artists, and scientists. The gardens have always been closely associated with the governing authorities, and have had a commemorative and cultural role: ever since the Renaissance, they have been a venue for many festivals, ceremonies, exhibitions, and events of every kind, some of which have gone down in history, and others that have been quite extraordinary. By exploring some of the major events in the history of France and presenting readers with unusual images and surprising quotations, this book is a mine of information to visitors—regular and occasional visitors to the gardens, and those who believe they are already familiar with the Tuileries or are discovering them for the first time.

———————

CONTENTS

2. Robert Holmes (1943–), *The Garden in Flower in the Summer after the Renovation Work by Pascal Cribier and Louis Benech*, 19 June 1996.

3. 'Plateau-pruned' mulberry trees, near trampolines, 2007. Paul Belmondo (1898–1982), *Apollon* ('Apollo'), 1933, bronze, on permanent loan from the Centre National des Arts Plastiques.

THE RENAISSANCE
SPLENDOUR

4. François Clouet (1520–1572), *Portrait of Catherine de' Medici,
Queen of France* (detail), before 1572, coloured pencil, black chalk,
and heightened with sanguine, Department of Prints and Photographs,
Bibliothèque Nationale de France, Paris.

5. Brussels, after a cartoon by Luc de Heere and based on a drawing by Antoine Caron (1521-1599), *The Reception of the Polish Ambassadors by Catherine de' Medici in the Tuileries in 1573*, tapestry belonging to the *Fêtes des Valois* series (detail), circa 1582–1585, wool, silk, gold, and silver, Galleria degli Uffizi, Polo Museale della Toscana, Florence.

A garden in the Italian style

The Tuileries Gardens remain a model of garden design. It is essentially one of the first Italian-style gardens created in France during the Renaissance. Indeed, the garden was founded by none other than Catherine de' Medici. Educated in Florence and Rome, Catherine married the future king of France, Henry II, in 1533. Widowed in 1559, she devoted herself to governing the kingdom and commissioned the construction of a country residence, the Tuileries Palace, which was immediately complemented by a garden. Located to the west of the Louvre, outside the city's walls, the site owes its name the tile (*tuile*) factories and pottery workshops that exploited the alluvial soil deposited by flooding from the Seine.

6. The small southern reserved garden in the Grand Carré.
Roland Mathieu-Meusnier (1824-1896), *Death of Lais*, 1850, marble.

7. The Bernard Palissy tile-making kilns unearthed in the Tuileries
during the excavations for the reconstruction of the south wing,
9 August 1865, Musée Carnavalet – Musée d'Histoire de Paris, Paris.

THE TILE-MAKING KILNS DISCOVERED DURING THE GRAND LOUVRE EXCAVATIONS

Under the sculpture *Death of Lais* (1850) by Roland Mathieu-Meusnier, the excavations carried out in 1993 brought to light a sixteenth-century tile-making kiln. It is believed that it was capable of firing twenty thousand tiles per batch. This tile manufacturing industry probably occupied most of the area now covered by the Carrousel* and Tuileries Gardens, until Catherine de' Medici acquired the grounds.

Very little remains of this initial Renaissance garden, apart from the principle of a formal garden*: all the alleys that divide the garden into right-angle sections, which is why it was referred to as a 'regular garden'. Only the garden's perimeter has remained virtually unchanged. However, the original garden was not a perfect rectangle, but rather a trapezium, as there was a wall at the western end of the garden. This can be seen by visiting the Musée de l'Orangerie: an invaluable bastion, uncovered in 2003, has been conserved in the museum's basement. It was a major element of the Fossés Jaunes (yellow moats) enclosure, which was designed to protect Catherine de' Medici's palace and garden and whose construction began in 1565.

8. The Fossés Jaunes (yellow moats) enclosure: part of a bastion discovered under the Musée de l'Orangerie in 2003 and reconstructed *in situ*.

Although the garden was completed in 1573 and was used to host various festivities, the construction of the palace was interrupted and the symmetrical layout* of the edifice, which was designed to have a central pavilion with wings, was never taken to its conclusion.

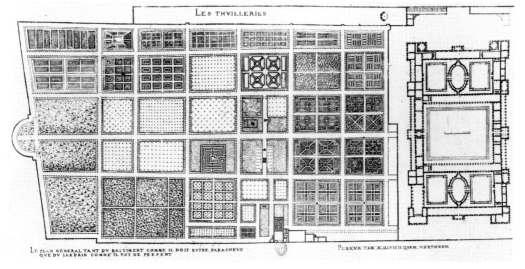

9. Jacques I Androuet du Cerceau (circa 1515 – 1585), *The Tuileries: an Overall Plan of the Final Building and the Garden in its Current Layout*, 1579, etching, in *Les Plus Excellents Bastiments de France* ('The finest buildings in France'), 1607, Department of Prints and Photographs, Bibliothèque Nationale de France, Paris.

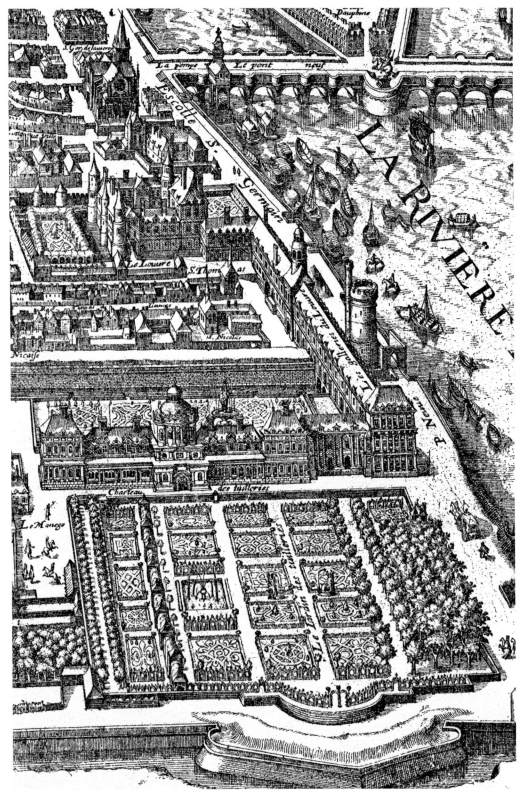

10. Mathieu Merian (1593–1650), *Map of Paris* (detail), 1615, Department of Prints and Photographs, Bibliothèque Nationale de France, Paris.

BERNARD PALISSY'S GROTTO

Palissy's grotto was an extravagant and entirely man-made decorative work. The walls were made of artificial stones, which were covered in moss and lichen, and the grotto was filled with shells and animals; male and female figures were housed in niches. All these objects were made of 'terre cuicte esmaillée' ('glazed terracotta'). Inside Bernard Palissy's workshop, which was discovered under the Carrousel garden, numerous experimental pieces were found, based on moulds that were used to record the shapes of many real animals—such as snakes, lizards, and frogs— as well as highly coloured and brilliant relief works. The grotto quickly fell into ruin and eventually disappeared, and its exact location remains a mystery.

11. Bernard Palissy (circa 1510 – 1589 or 1590), Frog: a fragment of brick with many alveoli created for the Tuileries grotto, circa 1570, Musée National de la Renaissance, Écouen.

The garden in Henri IV's capable hands

At the end of the sixteenth century, the garden suffered extensive damage during the Wars of Religion and from flooding. When Henry IV conquered Paris in 1594, he took care to restore the garden and commissioned the construction of the Bord-de-l'Eau Gallery, which linked the Tuileries Palace to the Louvre. The mulberry trees in the Grand Carré* evoke a remarkable innovation, which was devised by the agronomist Olivier de Serres and supported by the Good King Henry: the introduction of these trees, which can be used for rearing silkworms, throughout the kingdom. In the Tuileries, the mulberry trees formed a long alley in the northern part of the garden, and the upholsterers, who used the silk, practised their craft in the Grande Galerie.

In the seventeenth century, the 'Thuilleries' Gardens—a spelling that was widely used at the time—continued to be reserved for the court. It is known that the little Louis XIII spent his entire childhood in the garden, where he played and hunted, shooting at crows with a harquebus, and learnt how to ride in the Manège, the covered riding school near the Tuileries Palace.

'Wednesday 28 [September]. — For dinner, he was served a quail, which he had captured on the hunt the day before, along with two sparrows, which he had killed in the morning and struck in the eyes, in the Tuileries, with his stone-bow.'

Jean Héroard's daily journals concerning the childhood and youth of Louis XIII, dated 28 September 1611.

12. Arnaud Chicurel (1963–), *The Octogone Basin and the Grand Central Alley, with the Arc de Triomphe du Carrousel and the Louvre in the Background*, 21 September 2007.

THE SUN KING'S
GARDEN

For the glory of Louis XIV

In 1658, the estate was devastated by a flood of unprecedented proportions. This has been proved by archaeological probes conducted in 2012, which revealed the existence of a thick layer of silt. This flood explains why in 1664 Jean-Baptiste Colbert, Louis XIV's chief minister, entrusted the restoration of the garden to André Le Nôtre, who worked there from 1664 to 1671, while working in other gardens, and particularly at Versailles. Le Nôtre had a unique relationship with the Tuileries. Indeed, his grandfather and father had already worked in the garden—family gardening dynasties were common at the time—and he was born in the Tuileries in 1613. He lived in a house located in the north-eastern corner of the Tuileries—at the foot of the Marsan Wing of the Louvre—and died there in 1700. It could be said that Le Nôtre has continued to watch over the garden a long time after it was completed. The Tuileries are one of Le Nôtre's most remarkable creations. However, they are very much based on Catherine de' Medici's garden. The principle of a regular grid was maintained, but the entrances and perimeter

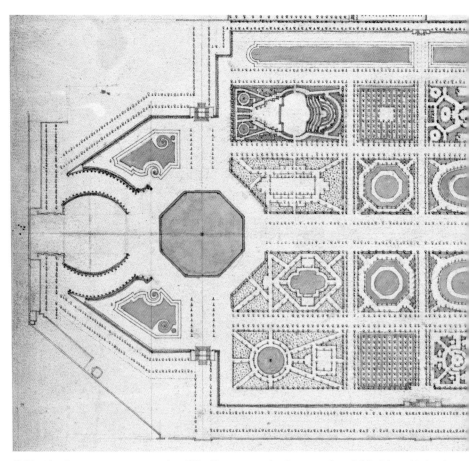

13. The 'des Capucins' survey map, after 1673, département des Cartes et plans, Bibliothèque Nationale de France, Paris.

were enhanced and embellished, and an axis ran between the central pavilion of the Tuileries Palace, which the architect Louis Le Vau had recently completed, and the end of the garden in the west. Le Nôtre's stroke of genius in the Tuileries was that he opened up the perspective towards the distant horizon: he created the Avenue des Champs-Élysées and extended it to the west up to Saint-Germain-en-Laye. The view of those strolling in the garden was no longer blocked by a wall but extended towards the horizon, between the two terraces in the north and south. Hence, the Tuileries were more than just a garden: by recreating the garden, Le Nôtre created a central axis, which laid the foundations for urban planning in Paris. Furthermore, the garden was opened to the public, or at least certain members of public, because the servants and ordinary soldiers were, for example, excluded from entry. The garden was a resounding succes. Althought the king moved his royal court to Versailles, the Tuileries were highly prized by the Parisians, and ever since the gardens have been an enduring success.

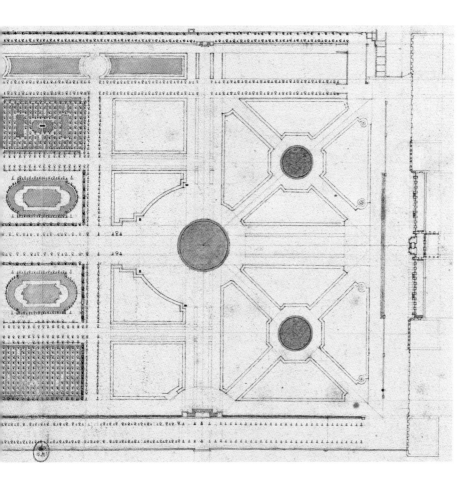

THE ESTATE'S LACK OF ALIGNMENT

Due to the meandering form of the River Seine, it was not possible to align the Louvre and Tuileries Palaces. There is, in fact, a lack of parallelism between the buildings. The Louvre Palace, from the Colonnade to the Pyramid, is built on an axis that deviates some 6 degrees north-west from the Carrousel Arc de Triomphe. This is immediately evident to any person entering the Tuileries from the Concorde end of the garden: the perspective of the grand central alley does not lead straight to the Pyramid. The axis of the Tuileries is indicated by the presence of Bernini's statue of Louis XIV, which was installed by Ieoh Ming Pei in the Cour Napoléon, in front of the Pyramid.

14. Hervé Bernard (1958–), *The Central Alley in the Tuileries Gardens, with Ieoh Ming Pei's Pyramid and the Louvre in the Background*, 2012.

15. *The Perspective of the Grand Central Alley Leading to the Place de la Concorde, the Champs-Élysées, the arc de triomphe de l'Étoile, and La Défense*, 2012.

16. Nicolas Pérelle (1631–1695), *Contemporary View of the Tuileries Gardens*, 1680, etching, Musée National des Châteaux de Versailles et de Trianon, Versailles.

17. Nicolas Pérelle (1631–1695), *View of the End of the Grand Central Alley in the Tuileries Gardens*, circa 1670, etching, Musée National des Châteaux de Versailles et de Trianon, Versailles.

Composition and illusion

Le Nôtre's enduring imprint is still evident in the structural layout* of the grounds, thanks to the phenomenal landscaping and levelling work, the extent of which we can no longer fully appreciate today. However, it can be seen when one observes the Bord-de-l'Eau terrace: it appears to be sunken, but it is important to remember that the ground was almost a metre lower. Le Nôtre's enduring imprint remains strong in the garden's architectural elements. In the south, the Bord-de-l'Eau terrace serves as a dyke against the whims of the river, while offering people strolling in the gardens an elevated viewpoint over the Seine and the garden. In the north, the Feuillants terrace—named after a convent that no longer exists—is still there, with its long esplanade, even though the creation of the Rue de Rivoli under the Empire took part of it away and it is no longer as green as it was in the eighteenth century. In the west, horseshoe-shaped ramps ornamented with topiaries* and striking sets of steps lead to these terraces. The basins animated by jets of water, created by Le Nôtre, are still there: three round basins close to the palace and a large octagonal pond at the west end; the proportions of the basins have been calculated in such a way that, visually, they appear to be of the same size and shape. But this optical illusion, created to be viewed from the noble floor (first floor) of the central pavilion, at a height of around ten metres, can no longer be experienced, because the Tuileries Palace no longer exists. The central alley continues

18. *The Bord-de-l'Eau Terrace Seen From the Pavillon de Flore*, 2012.

19. The Octogone's southern steps. On the plinth: Henry Moore, *Reclining Figure*, 1951, bronze, on permanent loan from the Musée National d'Art Moderne – Centre Pompidou.

to offer visitors the splendour of its perspective view. The symmetrical nature of the garden's layout is particularly striking. Everything is arranged on either side of the central alley: each flower bed* and grove has a counterpart, which makes the garden easy to apprehend. However, this symmetrical layout is not monotonous, because the counterparts are not always an exact copy. If one explores each grove, one realises that none of them are alike, when compared with their symmetrical counterparts or the groves nearby. Le Nôtre's general layout, with its two distinct parts, has also been maintained: under Louis XIV, visitors walked down from the palace into the garden and arrived at an open area, called

20. Nicolas Langlois (1640–1703), *Plan of Four Copses in the Tuileries Gardens*, top right: the open-air theatre, circa 1690–1700, etching and engraving, Department of Prints and Photographs, Bibliothèque Nationale de France, Paris.

MONUMENT TO CHARLES PERRAULT

The author of famous tales, Charles Perrault was also Colbert's right-hand man. He wrote in his memoirs that hardly had the work on the gardens been completed, than Colbert wished to close them off, as he was worried that the general public would spoil the gardens 'in no time at all'. Perrault retorted and told him 'how much this garden is respected by everyone, even the most insignificant bourgeois. The women and children not only refrain from picking the flowers, but don't even touch them; everybody behaves quite impeccably'. These arguments persuaded Colbert to change his mind. The monument to Perrault commemorates his wonderful deed: children run around his bust, and the statuette of Puss in Boots evokes his literary talent.

the Grand Carré*, which contained *parterres de broderie** ('embroidered flower beds') enriched with a wide variety of flowers; then they arrived at the Grand Couvert*, a wooded area composed of sixteen copses* or 'small planted woods'; and, lastly, they reached the Octogone, the largest of the basins, and the Fer-à-Cheval, which is also an open area. This layout, which governs the progression of the walk, has remained unchanged. By contrast, the sophisticated flower beds with their well-defined motifs and the composition of the copses have not survived. Hence, an open-air theatre or greenery theatre* with terraces provided a setting for performances. But it only existed for a short period—around fifty years—because it was destroyed at the beginning of Louis XV's reign to make way for a pall mall walk for the young king. This area is still used as a play area with trampolines for children.

21. Gabriel Pech (1854–1930), *Monument Dedicated to the Storyteller Charles Perrault*, 1910, marble, on permanent loan from the Musée d'Orsay.

22. The Grand Degré and terrace of the Tuileries Gardens, 2007.
Pierre I Legros (1629–1714) and Jean Robert,
Two Vases Decorated with Garlands of Flowers and Rams' Heads, 1694, marble, Department of Sculpture, Musée du Louvre, Paris.

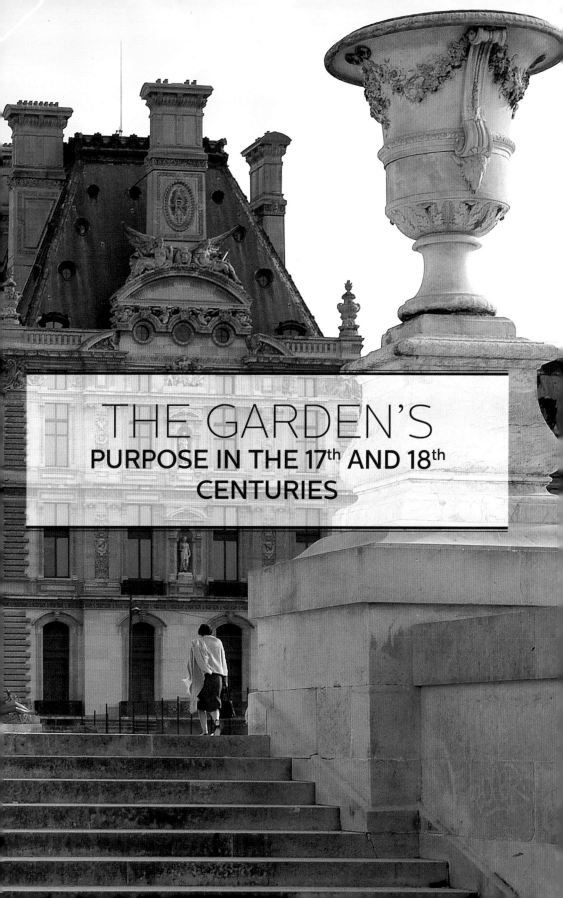

THE GARDEN'S
PURPOSE IN THE 17th AND 18th CENTURIES

Under the Regency

Although the development of the garden's purpose explains the disappearance of certain features, the costs and difficulties associated with its maintenance were also important factors. When Louis XIV died in 1715, the kingdom was riddled with debts and the regent of France, Philippe II, duc d'Orléans, had to take decisive action. A garden is expensive to maintain. And, in the eighteenth century, the trees planted by Le Nôtre—numerous horse chestnut trees, which were considered very exotic—matured and aged: they became difficult to prune and, indeed, many of them were felled. The topiaries*, which were very expensive to maintain, were not systematically replaced. The planted area decreased in size. Although many sculptures were added in 1716, transferred in particular from the garden of Marly, and the flower beds* and alleys were ornamented and punctuated with vases and stone benches of superb quality, there was, to our knowledge, very little by way of innovation in the garden. The garden gradually lost its homogeneity and novelty, just as it ceased to be of interest to the ruling authorities. In 1722, Louis XV returned to Versailles, taking with him his family and the royal court. His descendants did not spend their childhood in the Tuileries. It was only in 1789 that Louis XVI, who had only ever been familiar with Versailles, returned—compelled and forced by the people—to live in the Tuileries with his wife Marie-Antoinette and their children, including the young dauphin.

Marly was a leisure property, with gardens decorated with statues, that was built by Louis XIV near Versailles so he could take respite from the Court.

STATUES AND VASES FROM VERSAILLES AND MARLY

Certain sculptures that adorned the gardens of the royal domains were transferred to the Tuileries at the beginning of the eighteenth century. Hence, the monumental vases standing on either side of the Grand Degré, at the eastern entrance, came from the Orangerie in Versailles. At the Concorde end, the two groups carved by Coysevox to proclaim the glory of the Sun King were transferred from the Marly gardens, where they stood on either side of the Abreuvoir basin. This process continued up until the Revolution, and included, amongst others, the statues known as the 'Coureurs de Marly', placed in the exedrae. Transferred to the Tuileries in 1719, Coysevox's original sculptures were housed at the Louvre and their copies paced in the garden in 1986. A visit to the spectacular Cour Marly in the museum gives the visitor an idea of the sheer magnificence of the carved decorations in the royal gardens during the reigns of Louis XIV and Louis XV.

23. Antoine Coysevox (1640–1720), *Fame Mounted on Pegasus*, cast after the original in marble dating from 1702 and held in the Department of Sculpture, Musée du Louvre, Paris.

The rotating bridge and the Place Louis XV

Two innovations date from the eighteenth century. Firstly, the possibility of entering the garden from the west. Indeed, although Le Nôtre had opened up the perspective towards the Champs-Élysées, a deep trench, or ha-ha*, formed an insurmountable boundary. In 1716, an ingenious rotating bridge provided access during the day, but was closed at night. And, under the reign of Louis XV, a vast square was designed by the architect Ange Jacques Gabriel; it contained an equestrian stature of the monarch, erected in 1763, and was surrounded by moats on all sides. After the Terror, it became the Place de la Concorde; the obelisk originating from Luxor and offered by Mohammed Ali, viceroy of Egypt, did not arrive until 1836, together with the statues representing various French cities and the fountains that continue to ornament the square; and the moats were only filled in under the Second Empire.

24. Anonymous, *The Bord-de-l'Eau Terrace Steps* (detail), circa 1760, watercolour drawing, Musée Carnavalet – Histoire de Paris, Paris.

Le Nôtre's work did, however, survive well into the eighteenth century. During the reigns of Louis XV and Louis XVI, the Tuileries remained a very popular promenade, where people 'of quality' and 'refined' people, as they say, came to see and be seen, talk business, speak of love, or politics, enjoy a walk in the fresh air and meet people. They were all admired by travellers.

25. François Huot (late 18th century – early 19th century), *Politicians Reading the Newspapers in the Tuileries Gardens*, circa 1780, watercolour drawing, Department of Prints and Photographs, Bibliothèque Nationale de France, Paris.

'I was struck by the extraordinary sight as I approached the Tuileries! I saw an immense and unique garden; it stretched out before me, and my eyes were incapable of assessing its extent; I hurried through its alleys, copses, terraces, and flower beds; I beheld luxurious gardens, superb buildings, and precious monuments: nothing can equal the magnificence of the Tuileries.'

Carlo Goldoni (1707-1793), *Memoirs of Mr Goldoni to Serve The Story of His Life and That of His Theatre*, written in 1784–1787, published in 1822.

Experience du Globe Aërostatique de M.M. Charles et Robert,
Devant le Chateau des Thuileries,   le 1. x.^bre 1783. à 1. heure 40 minutes.

Ils descendirent à 3 heures ¾ dans la prairie de Nesle à 9. Lieues de Paris, ou M.^r le Duc
de Chartres et M. le Duc de filz-James signerent un proces verbal. M. Charles reparti
seul à 4 heures ¼, s'est elevé à 1524 toises évaluées par le Baromettre; ensorte qu'il à
passé de la temperature du printems à celle de l'hiver. il à mit pied à terre au bout
de 35 minutes dans les friches du bois de la Tour du Lay à 1. lieue ½ de Nesle.
            M. de Montgolfier, fit partir un petit Globe Verd qu'on perdit de vue en 5. Minutes.

26. *The Aerostatic Balloon Experiment Conducted by Messrs Charles and Robert*, 1783, watercolour etching, British Library, London.

27. Maurice-Louis Branger (1874-1950), *Young Women Near the Basin of the Tuileries Gardens*, circa 1925, gelatine silver-bromide glass negative.

28. Gérard Jean-Baptiste Scotin (1671-1716), after Jean de Saint-Jean (1655? – 1695), *Mesdemoiselles Loison Strolling in the Tuileries*, extract from the *Livre curieux des modes sous Louis XIV* ('The curious book of fashions under Louis XIV'), 1694, Department of Prints and Photographs, Bibliothèque Nationale de France, Paris.

AN INSPIRATION FOR FASHION

From the seventeenth century onwards, the Tuileries became a venue for displaying the latest fashions. It was here that people showed off their finest attire, and it also provided the setting for works that launched clothing trends, such as the *Livre curieux des modes sous Louis XIV* ('The curious book of fashions under Louis XIV'). Photographers subsequently often used the Tuileries as a setting for photos, like these two young women standing in front of the round basin. Various events are now held on the Esplanade des Feuillants to promote French fashions.

29. Southern exedra.
On both ends of the bench: François Masson (1745–1807), *Chimeras*, marble, 1798. On the plinth: Pierre Lepautre (1659–1744), *Faune au chevreau* ('Faun with kid'), cast after the original in marble dating from 1685 and held in the Department of Sculpture, Musée du Louvre, Paris.

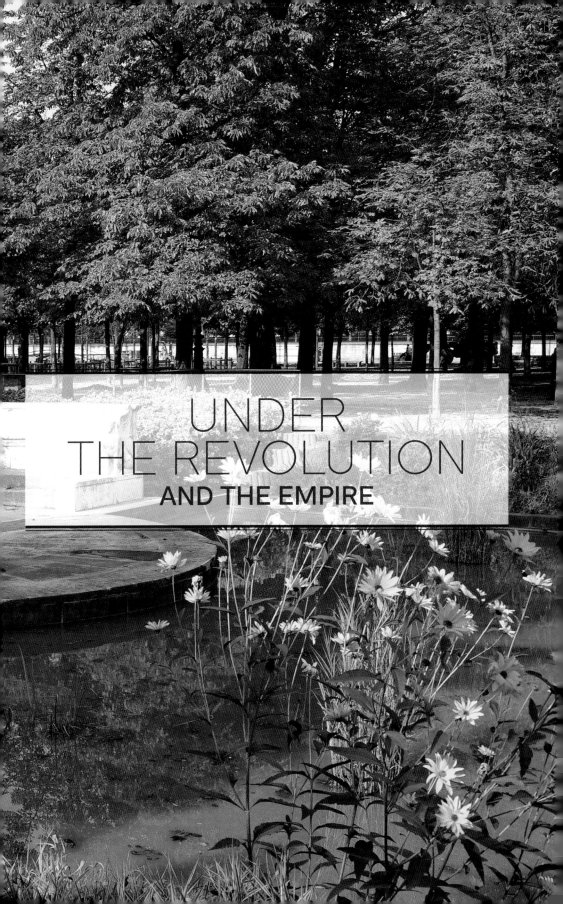

UNDER
THE REVOLUTION
AND THE EMPIRE

The people's garden

The Parisians seized the Tuileries Palace during the Revolution. The garden became a 'national' park, and the Louvre became known as the Musée Central des Arts in 1793. Because of its vast open spaces and its location near the major revolutionary centres—the Salle du Manège and the Club des Jacobins—there were both riots and festivities there.

30. Anonymous, *The Young Patriot* or *The Royal Family in the Tuileries*, 1790–1791, watercolour etching.

31. Hubert Robert (1733–1808), *The Cenotaph of Jean-Jacques Rousseau in the Tuileries* (detail), 1794, oil on canvas, Musée Carnavalet – Histoire de Paris, Paris.

All sorts of redevelopment projects, which were often utopian, were proposed. All that remains of them are the *exedrae*, works in stone entrusted to the architect François Masson and the sculptor Jean Charles Alexandre Moreau. The term refers to a semi-circular stone bench, which is very architectural in design; the form is based on the exedrae produced in Roman antiquity, in this case an element that was discovered during archaeological excavations conducted in Pompeii at the end of the eighteenth century. Hence, the Tuileries were ornamented with works in the Pompeiian style and imbued with neoclassicism; however, oblong basins were added, which are very different from those of Le Nôtre, because they offer a form of meditative intimacy and are in a pre-Romantic style. The construction of the exedrae was carried out between 1794 and 1798, shortly before Bonaparte came to power.

REVOLUTIONARY FESTIVALS

The year 1794 was a particularly eventful one, with the 'Festival of Saltpetre', on 10 March, the 'Feast of the Supreme Being', on 8 June, and the funereal tribute to Jean-Jacques Rousseau on the night of 10 to 11 October. The writer and philosopher of the Enlightenment had, in fact, died in 1778. In April 1794, the Convention ordered his ashes to be transferred to the Panthéon. An urn was exhibited in a small temple in the middle of a man-made island placed in the Octogone basin, in order to evoke the great man's initial sepulchre on the Île des Peupliers at Ermenonville (Oise), and has a great impact on the many spectators who come to pay tribute to him.

32. Étienne Barthélemy Garnier (1759–1849), *The Bridal Procession of Napoleon I and Marie-Louise Crossing the Tuilerie Garden, 2 April 1810* (detail), 1810, oil on canvas, Musée National des Châteaux de Versailles et de Trianon, Versailles.

NAPOLEON'S MARRIAGE IN 1810

To celebrate his marriage with Archduchess Marie-Louise of Austria, Napoleon organised sumptuous events. As the religious ceremony was held in the Louvre, the procession arrived from the Place de la Concorde and crossed the Tuileries Gardens. Fontaine designed exuberant scenery, comprising porticoes and arcades that embellished the entrance, adorned the grand central alley, and enhanced the pools. In the distance, at the top of the Champs-Élysées, is the arc de triomphe de l'Étoile, which, because it was as yet unfinished, was suggested by a wooden silhouette and painted canvas.
See previous double page.

An emperor in the Tuileries

Under the Consulate and the Empire, the northern end of the garden was transformed, with the creation of the Rue de Rivoli, which commences at the Place de la Concorde. Part of the Feuillants terrace was removed, but the northern end became more orderly and prestigious with its splendid iron railing ornamented with gilt spearheads—military terminology that is typical of the period— and its pillars, which were embellished with thirty-four Carrara marble Medici vases during the Restoration period. At the Concorde end, the terraces were bounded by stone balustrades, with lions in the corners.

PROMENADE DE S.M. LE ROI DE ROME,
Sur la Terrasse des Thuilleries.

33. Abel Blouet (1795-1853), *The King of Rome Playing in his Carriage in the Tuileries*, 1812, watercolour etching, Musée National du Château de Fontainebleau, Fontainebleau.

Napoleon used the garden as an instrument of power: his marriage was held there in 1810; this resulted in the widening of the central alley, and hence a decrease in the planted area. All these modifications were carried out by the architects Charles Percier and Pierre Léonard Fontaine. The emperor enhanced the axis created by Le Nôtre between the Arc de Triomphe du Carrousel, built in 1807–1809, and the Arc de Triomphe de l'Étoile, whose construction began in 1806, but which was completed in 1836. He did, in fact, live in the Tuileries Palace, whose splendour he restored. The Salle des Maréchaux, located in the central pavilion, offered a magnificent view of the Tuileries Gardens. The fall of the regime did not prevent Fontaine from remaining in his post until 1848.

34. The Sèvres Manufactory, a plate from the Emperor's personal dinner service with an illustration of the Tuileries Palace and the Rue de Rivoli, 1808, porcelain, Musée National du Château de Fontainebleau, Fontainebleau.

'It's a delightful dark promenade where one is sheltered from the heat, and above all from the glare of the sun, so trying in summer.'

Stendhal, preface of *Armance*, 1827.

35. The demilune ditch demarcating the northern reserved garden in the Grand Carré, 2010. Aimé Millet (1819–1891), *Cassandre Places Herself Under the Protection of Pallas*, 1877, marble, on permanent loan from the Musée d'Orsay.

A PUBLIC
AND PRIVATE GARDEN

36. Capitaine Cheret, *Review of the Troops in the Tuileries Gardens*, 1835, oil on canvas, Musée Condé, Chantilly.

The king's garden

However, under the July Monarchy, when Fontaine still had charge of the garden, and under the Second Empire, the garden open to the public was restricted to an area below the palace due to the creation of the 'reserved gardens'. Fearing mass riots and assassination attempts, King Louis-Philippe did, in fact, reserve a part of the garden for his own use. Fontaine even drew up plans to extend the palace by doubling the width of the façade, which would have encroached on the flower beds*. The foundations discovered during recent excavations have revealed that the work had been quite extensive. Although the work was interrupted, following strong criticism from the opposition, the gardens reserved for the king did extend to the small round basins or pools, forming a sort of buffer zone. Napoleon III went even further: he extended the annexation of the garden to the large round basin; a cluster of trees formed an elegant screen between

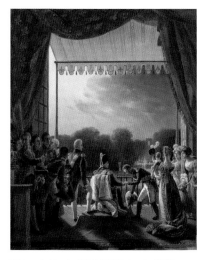

37. Louis Ducis (1775–1847), *Louis XVIII, Surrounded by Members of the Royal Family, Watches the Return of the Troops from Spain, 2 December 1823*, 1824, oil on canvas, Musée National des Châteaux de Versailles et de Trianon, Versailles.

the imperial family and the garden that was open to the public, and railings prevented access. Hence, this upset the balance of Le Nôtre's composition. The traces of the privatisation of the garden can still be seen: although the term 'reserved' is still used to refer to these areas of the garden, a ditch indicates their location, along the alleys, and the cluster of trees still exists, in which can be seen a conspicuous Corsica pine.

Sculpture and horticulture

To embellish the gardens, Louis-Philippe commissioned statues of great men and heroes of antiquity—statues that are now located in the Cour Puget in the Louvre and around the large round basin. Above all, he commissioned the *Lion and Serpent* by Antoine-Louis Barye.

38. Lancelot Théodore Turpin de Crissé (1782–1859), *Political Caricature: the Tuileries Ditch*, 1833, extract from *Paris à travers les âges* (*Paris Through the Ages*), Paris, 1875.

39. Étienne Jules Ramey (1796–1852), *Theseus and the Minotaur*, 1827, marble, Department of Sculpture, Musée du Louvre, Paris.

40. Antoine Louis Barye (1795-1875), *Lion and Serpent*, also called *Lion of the Tuileries*, 1836, bronze, Department of Sculpture, Musée du Louvre, Paris.

BARYE'S LION

Barye's statue of a lion crushing a serpent was a great success at the 1833 Salon. The symbol of strength and courage, the lion is a monarchical animal par excellence. Yet, with this work, Barye went beyond allegory and created an incredibly realistic, life-size lion, inspired by the big cats he closely observed in the menagerie of the Jardin des Plantes. Impressed by the formidable power of this piece, King Louis-Philippe commissioned a bronze copy, which he had installed in his reserved garden. The bronze version of the 'Lion des Tuileries' was placed in the Louvre in 1911 and replaced by a cement stone copy that was moved to a location near the Orangerie.

However, under the July Monarchy, the poor quality of the plant was criticized by the press. The Second Empire took a completely different approach, by introducing flowers and exotic trees, which grew with a certain exuberance. The nineteenth century was, after all, the century of horticulture. The development of transportation and the colonial conquests facilitated the importation of hitherto unknown plant species and horticulturists continued to create new varieties. Hence, the garden participated in the 'imperial festival'. Lastly, the last heir to the throne who spent his childhood in the Tuileries Gardens was the Imperial Prince. Born in the palace in 1856, he spent much time in the reserved gardens and the Bord-de-l'Eau terrace, until the fall of the regime in September 1870.

41. Charles Maurand (1824-1904), *HRH the Imperial Prince Riding on a Velocipede in the Reserved Garden of the Tuileries*, circa 1865, print, Musée National du Château de Compiègne, Compiègne.

Two edifices were built on the terraces between 1852 and 1862. Constructed on the Feuillants terrace, the Jeu de Paume still exists, as does its counterpart in the south, the Orangerie, but tennis and the storage of orange trees during the winter have given way to two museums that have recently been restored and reorganised.

42. Entrance of the Galerie du Jeu de Paume, 2007.

43. Entrance of the Musée de l'Orangerie, 2007. Auguste Rodin (1840-1917), *The Kiss*, 1898, bronze, on permanent loan from the Musée Rodin.

Painters and photographers

This period saw the emergence of a major innovation: photography. In the 1840s, the pioneers of photography focused their lenses on the Tuileries Palace and the garden, although the painters continued to set up their easels in the alleys. Manet used the garden as a basis for his pictorial revolution with *Music in the Tuileries Gardens*, painted in 1862. This was just the beginning of a practise that has continued to the present day. The garden, which for a long time featured on numerous postcards, is now one of the most represented places in Paris—in the works of world-renowned artists and in images produced by lovers of beautiful pictures and selfies.

44. Anonymous, *Stereoscopic View of the Reserved Gardens*, after 1857, private collection.

Ultimately, in the nineteenth century, when the Tuileries Palace became a centre of power once more, the original link between the edifice and the garden was strengthened.

Our two lordships
Repair to the Tuileries
Where they stroll
And make idle chatter
With the servants in pink
Under the chestnut trees.

[...] The white statues
In their state of undress
Display their breasts
With gestures so graceful
The envy of the swans
On the grand basin.

Victor Hugo, 'Les Tuileries', 1847.

45. Charles Nègre (1820-1880), *View of a Basin in the Tuileries Gardens*, 1859, wet collodion glass negative, Art Gallery of Ontario, Toronto.

46. Achille Quinet (1831–1907), *A View of the Tuileries Palace From the Garden*, 1868, albumenised paper print, Department of Prints and Photographs, Bibliothèque Nationale de France, Paris.

MANET'S *MUSIC IN THE TUILERIES GARDENS*

In this work, Manet painted a typical Sunday scene in the Tuileries Gardens, during a concert of military music. However, the orchestra is out of sight and the real subject is the dense and diverse crowd of onlookers, which contrasts with the garden's dark green chestnut trees. Here we see the reality of urban leisure during France's Second Empire. Yet, until that point, these scenes had only been depicted in the form of engravings published in the press. In 1862, it was unthinkable that this kind of scene might be represented in a painting. By challenging this notion, Manet became the 'painter of modern life', as Baudelaire expressed it—the poet is, in fact, portrayed in the painting, standing in profile behind the seated woman on the left— thereby opening the way for Impressionism.

See double page overleaf.

47. Édouard Manet (1832–1883), *Music in the Tuileries Gardens* (detail), 1862, oil on canvas, National Gallery, London.

48. Daniel Thierry (1951–), *Model Yachts at the Tuileries*, 2010.

THE BELLE ÉPOQUE

The garden is deprived of its palace...

The tragic event occurred in 1871: during the Paris Commune uprising, buildings were reduced to ashes and the old Tuileries Palace was destroyed by fire; the New Louvre, which had recently been completed by Hector Lefuel, narrowly escaped the fire. The building was first cleaned up by Lefuel, and then the connection between the Marsan Wing, to the north, and the Flore Wing, to the south, was removed, in order to reconstruct the pavilions. Finally, after more than ten years of procrastination, during which the ruins were an unsightly blot on the urban landscape, the palace was demolished and materials from the building were put up for sale. In the Tuileries there is an archway that is a vestige of the palace façade; it was designed by the architect Philibert Delorme and reconstructed in 2012. There are plans to reconstruct another archway, designed by Jean Bullant.

THE RUINS OF THE TUILERIES PALACE

Painters and photographers produced many fascinating images of the ruins of Catherine de' Medici's palace; they recorded the shock of the Parisians after the tragic event, as well as the treatment of the remains of the building for more than ten years, before their complete destruction.
This photograph is one of the rare ones to show how, from the vantage point of the Carrousel's Cour d'Honneur, the Tuileries Gardens could be seen, with the perspective view of the grand central alley. These photographs were an extension of the Western tradition of representing ruins in paintings. Their strange beauty invites the viewer to reflect on the ineluctable decadence of civilisations.

49. Fratelli Alinari, *The Ruins of the Tuileries Palace During the Purge*, 1871.

50. Camille Pissarro (1830–1903), *The Garden of the Tuileries on a Spring Morning*, 1900, oil on canvas, Museum of Fine Arts, Boston.

51. Édouard Vuillard (1868–1940), *The Tuileries Gardens*, circa 1894, oil on cardboard, Musée d'Orsay, Paris, donated by Jean-Pierre Marcie-Rivière.

THE CHESTNUT TREES

An exotic tree in Le Nôtre's era, the horse chestnut tree—which, in fact, originated in the Caucasus and Turkey—is now a very familiar sight. At the end of the nineteenth century, it was the main type of tree in the Tuileries, to such an extent that it was celebrated by many writers and artists, such as Émile Zola (*Au Bonheur des dames*, 1883) and the painter Édouard Vuillard. These days, chestnut trees are no longer planted: they are very sensitive to pollution and are decimated by diseases and parasites, such as bleeding canker and the horse chestnut leaf-miner, a voracious caterpillar that considerably weakens the trees.

.... but opened to the public

In the meantime, the Tuileries Gardens were reopened to the public and there was no longer any question of reserved gardens. Visitors walked along the palace's terrace and this naturally created a thoroughfare, which served as a north–south shortcut and became the garden's eastern entrance. It was called the Rue des Tuileries, and then, under the Third Republic, Rue Paul-Déroulède (today's Avenue du Général-Lemonnier). This raised the question of the future of the Cour du Carrousel. Edmond Guillaume, architect of the Louvre, transformed what had hitherto been a paved courtyard—used for military parades—into a garden. He created an exact copy of the old reserved gardens and embellished it with statues by living artists, which he obtained from public collections—works that conformed with the prevailing academic aesthetics.

52. Attributed to Gervais-Courtellemont (1863–1931), *The Musée des Arts Décoratifs at the Tuileries*, 1923.

53. A. Nardac, *The International Automobile Exhibition in the Tuileries*, 1898, colour lithograph, Paris, Automobile Club de France.

Guillaume wished to harmonise the entire garden, while modernising it. The way in which the flower beds* were organised conformed with aesthetics inspired by the work of landscape architects during the Second Empire. Hence, circular knolls were created with clusters of flowers; brightly coloured flowers formed spectacular clumps, which were sometimes used in mosaiculture (the art of using exotic plants and exuberant colour to create amazingly decorative gardens). This style, which was an awkward imitation of the work of the great garden designers during the Second Empire, continued to be used in the Tuileries and Carrousel gardens* until the 1970s. Of Edmond Guillaume's work as a landscape gardener in the Tuileries, only several sculptures remain.

FAIRS, EXHIBITIONS, AND EVENTS

Although everyone is familiar with the Universal Exhibition events, such as the banquet held by France's twenty-two thousand mayors in 1900, it is less well known that today's major exhibitions and fairs were first held in the Tuileries Gardens. In 1898, the first Automobile Fair was held at the Concorde end of the gardens; and, for a while, the Foire de Paris was held on the Esplanade des Feuillants. The gardens have hosted all sorts of events, from dioramas to dog shows, tethered balloons, races, and military exercises.

An urban park

The imperial garden, which had become a republican garden, was influenced by the parks and gardens created by Jean-Charles Alphand for the City of Paris during the Second Empire. As in the Buttes-Chaumont and Montsouris parks, various attractions and services developed at a rapid rate. The general public, which was essentially family-orientated, was attracted by the puppet shows and the merry-go round, the waffle and ice cream vendors, the donkey rides, and the carts drawn by goats. Although no edifice remains, apart from a cast-iron covered playground, there is still a large area to the north, near the Feuillants terrace, which is exclusively devoted to children, with an open-air playground, a merry-go round, and trampolines. The tradition of model yachts and regattas, which began in the nineteenth century, continues today.

THE MODEL YACHTS

The tradition of sailing model yachts goes back to the middle of the nineteenth century. It can be seen in popular engravings and in photographs from the time and featured on many postcards. Nowadays, children still play with these miniature boats in the northern pool, while once a year, in mid June, a regatta is organised on the Octogone pool. It could be said that this urban pastime, which evokes the activity of yachting, is an integral part of garden heritage, as are merry-go-rounds, which are reminiscent of the royal and aristocratic activity of horse riding.

54. *The Grand Bassin in the Tuileries Gardens,* circa 1900, postcard, private collection.

55. Anonymous, *Children and Nursemaids in the Tuileries Gardens,* circa 1894-1895, stereoscopic view.

56. Protection of the sculptures in the Tuileries Gardens, 1914.

'... And yet he had only really begun to feel this love the evening of their walk under the chestnut trees of the Tuileries. His life started from there, he could still hear the laughing of a group of little girls, the distant fall of a jet of water, whilst in the warm shade she walked on beside him in silence.'

Émile Zola, *Au Bonheur des dames (The Ladies' Paradise)*, 1883.

It was also during the Third Republic that cast-iron street furniture first appeared in the garden: street lamps—electricity was introduced in 1904—benches, public fountains, information panels, drain covers, and so on. On the eve of the First World War, Le Nôtre's 'formal garden'* became a Belle Époque and somewhat unexceptional urban park. Even political public monuments, which were part of the burgeoning 'statumania' of Paris, began to appear in the garden: a monument to Gambetta (in the Place du Carrousel), which was eventually destroyed, a monument to Jules Ferry (in the Esplanade des Feuillants), which is still in place, and another to Waldeck-Rousseau, which was recently moved below the Jeu de Paume. Nevertheless, an awareness of the garden's importance as a heritage site developed; it was classified as a historic monument in 1914, shortly before the outbreak of the First World War.

57. The snow-covered Tuileries Gardens, 2013.

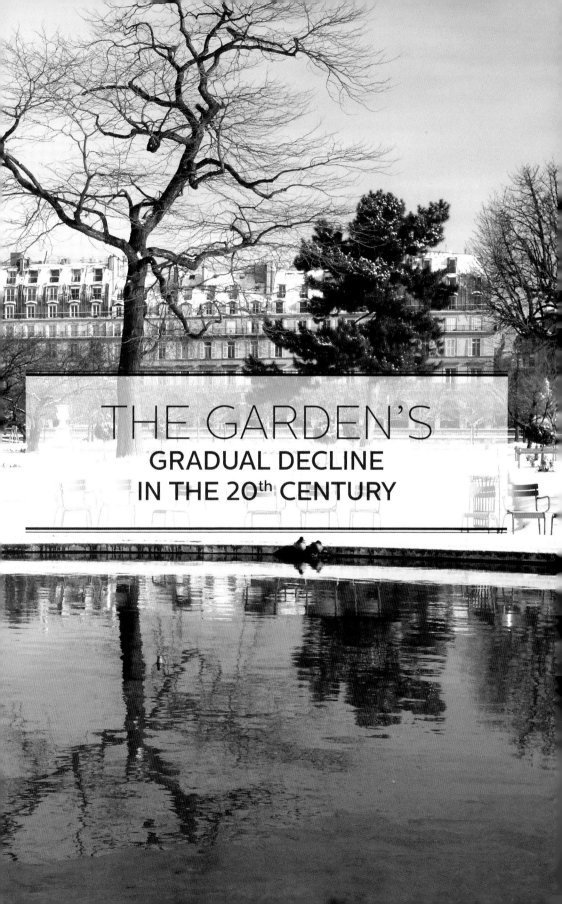

THE GARDEN'S
GRADUAL DECLINE
IN THE 20th CENTURY

58. Robert Doisneau (1912-1994), *Love and Barbed Wire*, 1944.

The garden was untouched by the war

Untouched by the two wars—the sculptures were protected with sandbags or buried in ditches and the few tank battles that took place during the liberation of Paris caused a few damage—little changed in the Tuileries Gardens until the 1950s. Only the Carrousel garden* was remodelled in the 1960s during André Malraux's period in office as French Minister of Cultural Affairs; he installed eighteen Aristide Maillol bronzes—which had been presented to France by the artist's model and executrix, Dina Vierny—on lawns that had been considerably simplified.

59. Burnt-out tank in the Tuileries, August 1944.

60. Aristide Maillol (1861-1944), *Grief*, 1922, bronze, on permanent loan from the Centre National des Arts Plastiques.

MAILLOL
AT THE CARROUSEL

In 1964, the French State received a donation of an ensemble of sculptures by Aristide Maillol (1861–1944). It was Dina Vierny, the artist's model and executrix, who managed to convince André Malraux, the Minister of Culture, to turn the Carrousel garden into an open-air Maillol museum. The pieces were officially donated by Lucien Maillol, the artist's son, but the installation work was organised by Dina Vierny herself. In 1995, even though the new garden was not yet finished, she rearranged the works. The museum was opened in October, shortly before the inauguration of the Fondation Dina Vierny–Musée Maillol, in Rue de Grenelle.

'[...] the mysteries of the Louvre courtyard, the two squares of the Carrousel, and the Tuileries, where my brother and I spent long afternoons. Black stone and leaves from the chestnut trees in the sun. The theater of greenery. The mountain of dead foliage against the foundation wall of the terrace, underneath the Musée du Jeu de Paume. We assigned numbers to the alleyways. The empty basin. [...] The green pair of scales against the wall of the Terrasse du Bord de l'Eau. The ceramic and coolness of the "lavatory" underneath the Terrasse des Feuillants. The gardeners. The rumble of the lawnmower engine, one sunny morning, on the grass near the basin.'

Patrick Modiano, *Pedigree: A Memoir*, 2015.

61. Anonymous, *Three young children riding donkeys in the Tuileries Gardens*, 1957.

62. Dmitri Kessel (1902–1995), *Aerial View of the Louvre and the Tuileries Garden*, an assignment for *Life*, 1953.

The decline in peacetime

Paradoxically, the return to peace had a negative impact on the garden. A series of popular events and festivals were held in the Tuileries, causing widespread damage and deterioration. Created in 1948 to support the social welfare activities carried out by General Leclerc's Second Armoured Division, the 'Kermesse aux Etoiles' ('Carnival of the Stars') enabled the general public to encounter their stars of cinema and song. Stalls, refreshment stalls, and performances proliferated, attracting a packed crowd of onlookers—which was difficult to control—for a period of three days and nights. The fans approached their idols to obtain autographs. The 'Fête des Tuileries' funfair began at the beginning of the 1970s. Even the French Revolution bicentennial (1989) was an insignificant event, in spite the quality of the 'Tours de la Liberté' ('Towers of Liberty') built by architects Jean-Marie Hennin and Nicolas Normier. The garden's classification as a historical monument proved to be a failure, because the budget devoted to the garden's maintenance was derisory. Disheartened, the gardeners stopped planting in the flower beds*, because the plants were stolen or damaged by the visitors. The sculptures were deliberately or unintentionally vandalised. A series of reports were drafted, which sounded the alarm bell: it was high time the garden was restored to its erstwhile splendour and, above all, given real meaning.

63. Anonymous, *A stand at the 'Carnival of the Stars'*, 14 June 1949.
From left to right: Jean Martinelli, Jean Gabin, Jean Pierre Aumont, and Claude Dauphin.

64. An advertisement for the VéloSoleX S. 2200, 1961.

A TELEPHONE EXCHANGE UNDER THE GARDENS

In 1971, as part of the initiative to modernise telecommunications, the French state decided to excavate the southern section of the Grand Carré* in order to install a telephone exchange over a surface area of 8,500 m². This equipment handled the intense telephone traffic of central Paris and paved the way for the introduction of touch-tone telephones. However, the works overseen by the palace's architect Marc Saltet caused some contention. Nevertheless, a stamp was issued to celebrate this curious association of heritage and technology.

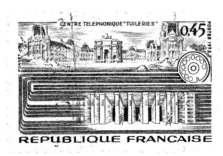

66. Pierre Forget (1923-2005), stamp featuring the 'Tuileries Telephone Exchange', 1973, soft-ground etching.

65. Hervé Bernard (1958–), *The Bicentenary of the French Revolution*, 1989.
In the foreground: Laurent Marqueste (1848–1920), *The Centaur Nessus*, 1892, marble, on permanent loan from the Centre National des Arts Plastiques.
In the background: one of the Liberty Towers.

67. Hervé Bernard (1958–), *Blooming Judas Tree in the Tuileries*, 2010.
Aimé Millet (1819–1891), *Cassandra Places Herself Under the Protection of Pallas*, 1877, marble, on permanent loan from the Musée d'Orsay.

THE NEW LIFE
OF THE TUILERIES GARDENS

An ambitious project

In September 1981, President François Mitterrand launched the Grand Louvre project and announced his intention to restore the gardens. Under the aegis of Jack Lang, Minister of Culture in 1981–1986 and 1988–1993, an awareness of the importance of garden design—from the point of view of heritage and contemporary design—developed in governing bodies. A series of specialist advisers came and went, such as Marc Simonet-Lenglart and Nelly Tardivier. It was not until 1990 that a competitive tender was launched. Eight candidates were selected and they were divided into two teams: the Tuileries were entrusted to landscape architects Pascal Cribier and Louis Benech, who were assisted by Monique Mosser, a garden historian, and François Roubaud, an architect; the Carrousel garden* was entrusted to the Belgian landscape architect Jacques Wirtz, who was assisted by his son Peter. Ieoh Ming Pei, the architect who designed the Grand Louvre, created a terrace between the two gardens that covered the Avenue du Général-Lemonnier, which became an underground passage. Nothing evoked the presence of the former palace.

PASCAL CRIBIER
(1953–2015)

The renovation of the Tuileries Gardens launched the careers of its designers. Having passed away prematurely in 2015, Pascal Cribier was one of the most important landscape architects of the end of the twentieth and early twenty-first centuries. He designed more than one hundred and eighty gardens, including *ex nihilo* creations and the redesign of existing gardens. Some noteworthy examples are Méry-sur-Oise (Val-d'Oise), Vez (Oise), Aramon (Gard), and Woolton House in England (Hampshire), not forgetting that of the Centre Pompidou-Metz (Moselle) and his own garden in Varengeville-sur-Mer (Seine-Maritime).

68. The competition winners (detail), 12 April 1994.
From left to right: François Roubaud, Pascal Cribier, and Louis Benech.

69. Hervé Bernard (1958–), *The Excavation Work in the Grand Carré*, 1992.

70. Springtime in the reserved gardens of the Grand Carré, 2007.

The palimpsest garden

The plan retained by the Cribier-Benech team did not consist of restoring the garden to its Le Nôtre state, whose exact form was not known, and which only existed for a very short period and, above all, was no longer suitable for the garden's high number of visitors. The aim instead was to integrate the successive transformations by conserving their traces as much as possible, while giving the garden a sense of unity. This is known as a 'palimpsest garden'. Hence, the exedrae, which were inherited from the Revolution but were covered in grass and in a poor condition, were integrated into a basin, which restored some of their original sense of harmony. Likewise, the ditches indicating the boundary of the reserved gardens were maintained, as were the large and medium-sized trees in the Grand Carré*, such as the Judas trees, whose pink flowers are a veritable feast for the eyes in springtime. The Grand Couvert* was not completely restored: the diseased trees and those that had reached the end of their life were simply felled, and then replaced by healthy trees, and the alignments were re-established along the Esplanade des Feuillants. No replicas of Le Nôtre's 'embroidered' flower beds* were created, but flower beds enabled the gardeners to express their creativity in the Grand Carré.

The extensive work on the garden was carried out over ten years. Archaeological excavations were conducted behind the palisades*, mainly in the Carrousel garden*; the ground was levelled, without reverting back to the seventeenth-century level, but enough to ensure that when visitors to the Louvre descended the steps they found some peace and quiet, away from all the noise of the traffic; eight hundred of the three thousand trees were felled and replaced; the sculptures in the Grand Carré were restored and regained a sense of coherence; the most fragile works were replaced by copies, and the original works were transferred to the Richelieu Wing, which was inaugurated in 1993; and kiosks, designed by Antoine Stinco, were installed for the vendors. The Carré du Sanglier remained an enclosed dry space without plants, as did the Esplanade des Feuillants.

THE CAMPAIGN TO RESTORE AND CREATE MOULDS OF THE SCULPTURES

The renovation of the gardens also resulted in the restoration of all the sculptures. The most damaged works were removed and are now housed in the Musée du Louvre, in the Cour Marly and Cour Puget in the Richelieu Wing, which opened in 1993. Some of them have been replaced by moulded replicas made from a mixture of synthetic resin and marble powder. While the garden was undergoing all the work, the statues were placed in a specific zone of the garden and the restorers carried out their work *in situ*.

71. Hervé Bernard (1958–), *Restored Statue Under Protective Cover*, 1995. Henri Vidal (1919–1959), *Cain After Killing his Brother Abel*, 1896, marble, on permanent loan from the Musée d'Orsay.

72. Élise Hardy (1962–), *Statue in the Tuileries Gardens*, 1992.
Denis Foyatier (1793–1863), *Cincinnatus*, 1834, marble, Department of Sculpture, Musée du Louvre, Paris.

Displays of contemporary art

In the meantime, the presence of sculpture in the gardens was studied; this assignment was entrusted to the sculptor Alain Kirili by the Minister of Culture Philippe Douste-Blazy and subsequently Catherine Trautmann, under the aegis of the French National Centre of Plastic Arts (CNAP). Modern and contemporary sculptures created by major artists were installed in the gardens in two phases, in 1998 and 2000. These works were permanent loans from private foundations and public institutions, such as the Musée Rodin, the Musée National d'Art Moderne and, of course, the CNAP itself, but it has also involved public commissions, the most spectacular of which was Giuseppe Penone's *The Tree of Vowels*, created in collaboration with Pascal Cribier and located in one of the southern copses*.

73. Giuseppe Penone (1947–), sculptor, in collaboration with Pascal Cribier (1953–2015), landscape architect, *The Tree of Vowels*, 1999, bronze, on permanent loan from the Centre National des Arts Plastiques.

GIUSEPPE PENONE: *THE TREE OF VOWELS*

Representing the *Arte Povera* movement, the Italian Giuseppe Penone built a profoundly humanist and poetic work, which is about our relationships with nature and time. A tree lies in the middle of an unusual grove, with wild plants consisting of ferns, Corsican hellebores, and Himalayan brambles; five different trees are growing on the tips of its branches. A passer-by might be forgiven for believing that it is a real tree, even though this oak tree is made of bronze. As it oxidises, the metal takes on the colour of tree bark. And its roots form vowel shapes, inspired by the poem 'Voyelles' by Arthur Rimbaud (1883) and *The White Goddess* and the *Celtic Myths* by the British poet Robert Graves (1948). Established by the landscape architect, the maintenance protocol of this copse is carefully followed by the Tuileries gardeners.

74. Hervé Bernard (1958–), *The Grand Carré in Summer Bloom*, 1996.

After being redesigned and rearranged, the gardens began a new phase of growth, which was subsequently hindered by climatic variations—notably the storm of December 1999, and the heat wave of 2003. Urban pollution, global warming, and spiking visitor numbers—the 1990 competition was launched at a time when an estimated six million people were visiting the gardens, which is now more like fourteen million—are all factors that are causing degradation. The soils are subsiding and are threatened with sterility, and the plants are finding it difficult to take root. The gardens' fragility is now becoming quite evident.

75. The Octogone: the orange trees and northern rose garden, summer 2015.

76. Fermob garden chairs and armchairs on the Bord-de-l'Eau terrace, 2010.

Channelling multidisciplinary skills into the maintenance of the gardens

The Tuileries Gardens are managed by the Musée du Louvre's Department for Architectural Heritage and Gardens, and since 2014, the running of the gardens has been entrusted to a single body—the Gardens Division. This encompasses the thirty hectares of the national estate, which comprises four other gardens (the Carrousel Garden*, and, to the east, the Oratoire, Infante, and Raffet gardens), not forgetting the Musée Eugène Delacroix garden. The preservation of these gardens depends on the collaboration of various companies with horticultural and technical expertise (to care for 3,000 trees, 6,000 square metres of flower beds*, and six basins), conservation (more than two hundred sculptures and vases), and managing maintenance. It also means that cultural events and regular and occasional shows need to be programmed. Applying the principles of horticultural engineering, the on-site team has multidisciplinary skills; this includes a heritage curator, an operations manager, and two managers specialising in plants. This multi-disciplinary approach provides adapted and creative solutions. The operations manager is responsible, in particular, for the maintenance work carried out by external companies, such as the ground maintenance, while the heritage curator works with sculpture

restorers, studies the history of the sculptures, as well as that of the gardens, and works to promote them through interpretation. Every day, seventeen artistic gardeners do their utmost to maintain the Tuileries and transmit the memory of their work and the site. All the work is carried out in close conjunction with the architect of the Bâtiments de France (ABF) and the architect-in-chief of the Monuments historiques, because the garden is classified as a historic monument. The Division works in conjunction with the Louvre's other engineers and external specialists. The lighting, watering networks, and water jets in the basins require constant maintenance, the signposts need to be replaced, and, above all, the site's cleanliness must be ensured—the many waste paper bins have to be emptied several times a day. And specialists are entrusted with diagnosing the health of the trees and analysing the chemical characteristics of the soil. The Gardens Division also works with associations to improve accessibility for people with disabilities and enable the fauna, especially the birds, to enjoy a comfortable life in the Tuileries. In any case, the factors of sustainable development and climatic change are taken into account. Hence, parasites are countered using auxiliary methods—bacteria, insects, and mites, which are all preferable to chemical products that represent a danger to people, the fauna, and the environment.

On the ground

The reception and surveillance staff consists of twenty or so agents. Every morning and evening, they are responsible for opening and shutting the garden's twelve entrances. During the day they tour the area on bikes to spot any dysfunctions and help visitors and tell them about behaviour that constitutes risks; this is quite a demanding job because of the large number of visitors, the long opening hours, and the large surface area of the estate.

77. The beds of the Grand Carré: manual weeding using a 'Grelinette', summer 2015.

Artistic gardeners require special training and are recruited to tend to historical state-run gardens. They carry out all kinds of work, from moving the lawns to making bird houses and the very delicate work involved in sizing the topiaries*. The larger and taller trees are, however, pruned, felled, and replanted by a specialist company. Thanks to the work of the gardeners, people strolling through the grounds can enjoy two floral displays per year: in the spring, from March onwards, and in summer between June and October. The flower beds change every year: prepared collectively, preparatory drawings are made, the appropriate plants are chosen, and detailed plans are drawn up. The planting periods are particularly intense, as are the periods during which the soil is prepared and mulch is spread to limit weed growth and reduce watering requirements. In hot weather, the plants need to be closely monitored.

78. A double row of orange trees to the north of the Octogone. The Jeu de Paume terrace is in the background, summer 2015.

THE ORANGE TREES

Adorning gardens with orange trees, lemon trees, and bitter orange trees in pots or boxes is a very old practice. There were many examples of this in Le Nôtre's gardens. While the Parisian climate does not produce fine fruit for those strolling through the gardens, as is the case in Mediterranean gardens, the sixty or so orange and lemon trees in the Tuileries Gardens do provide walkers with the beauty of their leaves and rounded forms. Because the Orangerie, which was built during the Second Empire, became a museum, the trees are taken to the Orangerie of the Domaine National de Meudon for the winter period. The Tuileries gardeners look after the trees with great care; they also paint the boxes in their characteristic fern green colour. In the summer, all the boxed trees are brought back to the Concorde entrance and around the Octogone basin.

These days, the gardeners also act as mediators: they provide guided tours for visitors who are curious to see behind the scenes and find out about how the grounds are run, during 'Rendez-vous aux jardins' gardening events and the European Heritage Days. Likewise, since 2006, the reception staff have been relating the gardens' history *in situ* every weekend during the summer.

79. A goat grazing in the ditch of the northern reserved garden. The Bord-de-l'Eau terrace is in the background, 2013.

ECO GRAZING

It is too dangerous for the gardeners to cut the grass in the ditches of the former reserved gardens due to the steep slopes. Hence, the practice of 'eco grazing' was introduced as a solution; this system uses goats or billy goats, which are brought to the site between April and October. These herbivores—from a breed of goats called the 'des fossés' (literally 'of the ditches')—originate from the Cotentin region of France. As their name suggests, they like to graze on sloping ground. They are given water and salt, their picket is moved regularly, and a covered area enables them to take shelter during bad weather. This practice has the added advantages of being ecological and sustainable.

'The gardeners work with living materials—plants—which do not appear to suffer in any way and whose death is sometimes even desirable. The gardeners are fortunate, as any sense of 'mourning' is entirely absent in the garden: they deal with the present and plan ahead for the upcoming seasons.'

Pascal Cribier, *Itinéraires d'un jardinier* ('A gardener's travels'), 2009.

80. Architectural pruning of the trees, autumn 2015.

81. Stéphane Ouzounoff (1960–), *Gardener at Work in the Southern Rose Garden*, 2007.

82. Arnaud Madelénat (1974–), *The North-East Copse and its Forest Beds*, 2012, gouache executed in preparation for the restoration conceived by Dominique Larpin.

THE FUTURE
OF THE GARDENS

83. Sophie Chivet (1962–), *The Garden Exhibition 'Jardins, jardin'*, June 2011.

An estate-based vision

Previously assigned to the Centre des Monuments Nationaux, in conjunction with the Palais-Royal, the management of the Tuileries Gardens was entrusted to the Musée du Louvre in 2005. This change of status brought obvious advantages, because, henceforth, the Louvre has been able to function as a single estate; a shared history has been complemented by a single management system. The Louvre's management subsequently called on the services of the garden specialist Nelly Tardivier, who then launched various projects, which were rapidly realised: creation of a playground in close collaboration with the Mairie of the first arrondissement, purchase of a stock of three thousand chairs, armchairs, and deckchairs, production of a new set of signposts and production of an archway coming from the Tuileries Palace.

The role of contemporary art has been consolidated since 2006 by hosting the 'Foire Internationale d'Art Contemporain' (FIAC) *extra muros*. Every year, in October, around twenty works are presented by various galleries, creating an amazing itinerary that attracts additional visitors to the Tuileries Gardens.

84. The Octogone Basin in the Tuileries.
Susumu Shingu (1937–), *Sinfonietta of Light*, 2012, installation comprising ten mobile floating elements, carbon fibre, aluminium, stainless steel and polyester, presented by the Galerie Jeanne Bucher Jaeger.

Continuing the process of renovation

In 2013, the Louvre was established to consolidate the quality and management of the estate's gardens. The 'master plan', a renovation plan that will continue the work already accomplished by Pascal Cribier and Louis Benech, focusing in particular on the replanting and diversification of the plant species. Entrusted to Dominique Larpin, the architect-in-chief of the Monuments Historiques, this master plan is based on a highly detailed historical study, this time underpinned by archaeological surveys directed by Anne Allimart-Verdillon, because the application of archaeology to the history of the gardens, as well as an analysis of practices, has made great progress over recent years. The emphasis will be placed on several large-scale projects: the restoration of the central alley's alignment, the renovation of the structures and grounds of the Fer-à-Cheval, complemented by replanting the walls and railings using climbing plants and topiaries, the restoration of the exedrae, including that of their surrounding trees, and the recreation of denser copses[*].

Experiments are also being carried out on the composition of soil, which was not resolved in a satisfactory manner in the 1990s. Of course, complete accessibility for persons with disabilities is another major priority, along with improving visitor services. The first phase of this master plan is underway, with the creation, since 2012, of a new copse: this involves the densification of the high hedges, deliberately varied tree species, the creation of forest beds that are designed to nourish the trees, with low hedges, and the quest for more permeable soils. This is the current state of play of research in the Tuileries Gardens. And in the Grand Carré*, the gardeners are experimenting with new floral arrangements for the flower beds and knolls, in conjunction with the exhibitions held by the museum. The tradition of innovation is continuing.

'The uncertainties of the future ultimately enable us to gain a better understanding of the subtle balances that are an integral part of the complexity of the living world. Gardening is about being sensitive to the world and the faintest of its rustles.'

Hervé Brunon, 'Pascal Cribier', in *Encyclopedia Universalis*, 2015.

85. The educational and ecological vegetable garden.
Anne Rochette (1957–), *Comptine : un, deux trois* ('Nursery rhyme: one, two, three'), 2000, patinated bronze fountain, three elements in painted bronze, and a painted iron fence, on permanent loan from the Centre National des Arts Plastiques.

86. Hervé Bernard (1958-), *The New Copse*, June 2015.
Erik Dietman (1937-2002), *L'Ami de personne* ('Nobody's friend'), 1998, bronze figure and steel chair, on permanent
loan from the Centre National des Arts Plastiques.

87. Wall of the Bord-de-l'Eau.
Philibert Delorme (circa 1510 – 1570), part
of the arcade with Ionic columns (built
between 1564 and 1570) from the façade
of the Tuileries Palace, Department of
Sculpture, Musée du Louvre, Paris.

THE NEW COPSE

Where there were only chestnut trees in a poor
condition a new copse was established. It houses
varied species, which require little water, are adapted
to climatic changes, and provide food for the birds.
In the centre, the cherry trees with their decorative
bark form a clearing, and there are maple trees with
spear-shaped, veined leaves, European hornbeam,
and service trees. At the foot of these trees, forest
beds filled with shrubs form a low shrub stratum,
which is adorned with perennials and bulbs.
Some of the plants were already used by Le Nôtre,
such as the honeysuckle plants that climb up
the tree trunks and the wire structures used to create
palisades*. Most of the plants selected are from
the Île de France region, like the wild tulip, *Angelica
officinalis*, and *Aspidia*, but the Rodgersia with horse-
chestnut leaves are rather exotic and the grasses
are contemporary in spirit. This floral fantasia
reflects the spirit of Le Nôtre, Cribier, and Benech.

88 and **89**. Arnaud Madelénat (1974–), *The Horseshoe Ramp with Topiaries and Palisades of Greenery; the Perimeter of the Octogone Adorned with Palisades and the Royal Alley Embellished with a Row of Trees*, 2012, gouaches executed in preparation for the restoration conceived by Dominique Larpin

GLOSSARY OF GARDEN TERMINOLOGY

Carré (the Grand)

The 'Grand Carré', which, in the Tuileries, corresponds to the open area, with its flower beds*, is not a true square. Indeed, in seventeenth-century France, the adjective 'carré' did not refer to a rectangle with equal sides, but rather applied to a square, rectangle, and lozenge. It derived its meaning from the Latin *quadratus*, meaning 'having four angles'.

Carrousel (Garden)

Pronounced ˌkarɔˈsɛl. Since the end of the 1880s, the Carrousel Garden has occupied the former Cour d'Honneur of the Tuileries Palace. It is located between the Louvre's two wings, that of Marsan in the north and Flore to the south. It is incorrect to refer to the Tuileries Gardens when mentioning the Carrousel Garden: the two gardens are quite distinct from one another. The word 'Carrousel' evokes the memory of a festival held by Louis XIV in 1662. A tournament was held there with magnificently attired horsemen, including the king himself. Today, the noun 'carousel' also designates a horse show or a merry-go-round of wooden horses.

Copse

The French word bosquet is derived from the Italian boschetto, meaning 'a small wood or cluster of trees'. The copses form the covered area* of a formal garden*. Composed of trees planted and shaped in a regular manner, they very often include a clearing or several open areas*, with statues, fountains, and other decorative elements. The plans of the Tuileries, which attest to Le Nôtre's compositional work, attest to the complex layout of the sixteen copses; this intricacy has now been lost.

Couvert (the Grand)

In the Tuileries Gardens, the 'Grand Couvert' refers to the middle area, which comprises sixteen copses*, in contrast with the 'Grand Carré'*. A regular garden* often includes a 'covered', wooded area, in which the trees provide shade and coolness, while in an 'open area' the flower beds* are exposed to the sun.

Embroideries

See 'Parterre'.

Enclosed area or rooms

The vocabulary of a regular garden* is often similar to that of interior architecture: when the plants—the lawn and the trees—are shaped in a certain way, they can form more enclosed rooms, salons, or *cabinets*, which were therefore more intimate and used for specific activities. The term 'salle verte' ('green area') is often employed, in contrast to a 'salle sèche' ('dry area'), which has no grass. The Tuileries Gardens have several enclosed 'green areas', and a single 'dry area', called the 'Carré du Sanglier' ('Wild boar's square'), in the gardens' south-west corner.

Flower bed

As indicated by its name, a flower bed is a flat, long and narrow strip of earth in an open area, intended for flowering plants, or even ornamental bushes that need to be exposed to the sun's rays. A knoll is similar to a flower bed but its surface is raised and rounded and is less long and more compact.

Formal (garden)

These days, the expression 'regular garden' is employed in French instead of 'jardin à la française' when designating a garden designed with compositional and symmetrical axes, in which geometry plays an important role. Thanks to this expression, it is possible to avoid attributing specific nations with the invention of a certain type of garden. Indeed it is not correct to contrast gardens 'à la française', inherited from Le Nôtre, with gardens 'à l'anglaise', which emerged in the eighteenth century, and which were, in fact, not an exclusively British invention.

Ha-ha or haha
This curious term designates a deep, waterless ditch that delineates a garden, while protecting it from intrusion and enabling those strolling in the garden to observe the horizon without being blocked by a boundary wall. A small ha-ha, limited to part of the garden, is also called a 'saut-de-loup' ('wolf's leap').

Layout (of the gardens)
This is the natural terrain on which the garden is located, with its relief, slopes, uneven terrain, and faults. The landscape architect's work is based on the analysis of this structural layout, which may subsequently be modified, thanks, in particular to levelling work.

Palisade
A palisade of greenery forms a sort of wall of greenery, thanks to its plants, which are shaped in a regular fashion. It can be used to embellish a wall, or even constitute a boundary wall on its own. In the Tuileries Gardens, there is a palisade of greenery formed by a bower, at the foot of the Pavillon de Marsan.

Parterre
This is a flat open area, on which are arranged shaped grass or 'embroideries', according to a pre-established design. The 'parterre de broderie' ('embroideries beds') derives its name from its ornamental characteristics: low pruned boxwood hedges forming scroll and arabesque motifs stand out against a coloured mineral soil, consisting of sand or gravel. The diverse forms of these motifs, along with the different thicknesses and heights of the boxwood hedges, make a bed more or less complex. Flowering or aromatic plants can also be added. To appreciate all the beauty of an embroidered bed, one needs to be able to observe it from a high vantage point, such as a terrace or balcony.

Theatre of greenery or open-air theatre
The expression designates an outdoor stage, on which performances are held in which plants play an architectural and decorative role. The very structure of a theatre of greenery is constituted of plants that grow in the ground. The fashion for theatres of greenery, from the mid seventeenth century onwards, was closely connected with the development of performances—theatre, opera, and ballet—under the reign of Louis XIV.

Topiary
A plant shaped decoratively using a template. The resulting forms may be geometrical or even figurative, and they are sometimes highly sophisticated. The trees or bushes shaped into topiaries add verticality to the parterres*; they punctuate and enhance the contours. At the Tuileries, topiaries of *Elaeagnus* planted along the grand central alley greet visitors strolling from the Louvre, while in the Carrousel Garden, skilfully pruned yew hedges are splayed out.

CHRONOLOGY

16th century

1564 The Tuileries Palace and Gardens are created for Catherine de' Medici, the widow of King Henry II.

1594 Henry IV restores the garden, which has been extensively damaged during the Wars of Religion.

—

17th century

1664 André Le Nôtre redesigns the garden for Louis XIV and opens up the perspective towards the Champs-Élysées.

1671 The completed garden is open to certain members of the public.

1700 Le Nôtre dies in the Tuileries.

—

18th century

1715 Louis XIV dies; Louis XV lives in the Tuileries Palace and returns to Versailles in 1722.

1716 The first marble sculptures are installed in the garden.

1789 Louis XVI and the royal family are compelled by the people to return to the Tuileries.

1793 The garden becomes a 'national' garden.

—

19th century

1801 Napoleon lives in the Tuileries and transforms part of the garden.

1831 Louis-Philippe reserves part of the garden at the foot of the palace for his own use.

1857 Napoleon III extends the reserved gardens.

1871 The Communards set fire to the Tuileries Palace.

1882 1883 The ruins of the palace are demolished; the Carrousel garden is created.

—

20th century

1914 The Tuileries Gardens are classified as a historic monument.

1964 1965 The Minister of Cultural Affairs, André Malraux, installs Maillol bronzes in the Carrousel garden.

1981 François Mitterrand, President of the Republic, announces the Grand Louvre project and the renovation of the gardens.

1990 1996 The garden is renovated by the landscape architects Pascal Cribier and Louis Benech; Jacques Wirtz recreates the Carrousel garden.

1991 The Tuileries Gardens are classified as a UNESCO World Heritage site, together with both banks of the Seine.

—

21st century

2005 The management of the Tuileries Gardens is entrusted to the Musée du Louvre.

2013 The master plan for the restoration of the Tuileries Gardens is approved by the Commission Nationale des Monuments Historiques.

2015 Pascal Cribier passes away.

2016 The new copse is completed.

KEY FIGURES

1
former tile
factory

2
terraces for walks

3
metro stations

4
coffee shops

6
basins

8
trampolines

10 t
of organic waste
per year

12
entrances

14
sets of steps

15
model yachts

17
gardeners

22,4 ha
of grounds

189
waste receptacles

213
statues and vases

555 m
the length of
the central alley

3,000
trees

3,000
chairs

5,785 m²
of flower beds and knolls

20,000
bulbs each year

14 000 000
visitors/walkers
per year

BIBLIOGRAPHICAL SECTION

(In inverse chronological order)

Emmanuelle HÉRAN, 'Les Tuileries, un jardin de toutes les époques. The Tuileries, A Contemporary Garden Through the Centuries.' (Emmanuelle Héran interviewed by Sarah Ihler-Meyer), in *Art Press* no. 427, November 2015, pp. 66–69

Exhibition catalogue, *The Art of the Louvre's Tuileries Gardens* (Atlanta, The High Museum of Art, 3 November 2013–19 January 2014; the Toledo Museum of Art, Toledo, 13 February–11 May 2014; the Portland Art Museum, Portland, 14 June–21 September 2014), Yale University Press, New Haven, 2013

Exhibition catalogue, *André Le Nôtre in Perspective* (Château de Versailles, Versailles, 22 October 2013–23 February 2014), Hazan, Paris, 2013

'The Tuileries Gardens', in *Connaissance des arts*, special issue, 2008

Emmanuel JACQUIN, *The Tuileries. From the Louvre to Place de la Concorde*, Éditions du Patrimoine/Centre des Monuments Nationaux, 'Itinéraires' collection, Paris, 2000

Online resources
www.louvre.fr
www.lenotre.culture.gouv.fr

PRACTICAL INFORMATION

Opening times

From 7:30 a.m. to 7:30 p.m., from the last
Sunday in September to the last Saturday
in March
From 7:00 a.m. to 9:00 p.m., from the
last Sunday in March to the last Saturday
in September
From 7:00 a.m. to 11:00 p.m., in June,
July, and August

Free tours

The general public (adults and children
aged 11 and over) on weekends and public
holidays, from 1 April to 1 November
Tours begin at 3:30 p.m. at the Arc de
Triomphe du Carrousel
*Tours may be cancelled in the event of a change
in the weather conditions*
Only in French

For further information consult: www.louvre.fr

Line 1, the Concorde, Tuileries,
or Palais-Royal – Musée du Louvre stations
Line 7, the Pyramides
or Palais-Royal – Musée du Louvre stations
Line 8, the Concorde station
Line 12, the Concorde station
Line 14, the Pyramides station

Line C, the Musée d'Orsay station,
then cross the L. S. Senghor footbridge

Lines 24, 48, 69 et 81

Vélib'
North of the Seine: 2 rue Cambon, 2 rue d'Alger,
5 rue de l'Échelle and 165 rue Saint-Honoré
South of the Seine, on the Left Bank: the quai
Anatole-France, then cross the L. S. Senghor
footbridge and the Quai Voltaire, and then cross the
Pont-Royal

Autolib'
North of the Seine: 3 rue Saint-Roch,
12 and 15 rue des Pyramides
South of the Seine, on the Left Bank: 5 Rue de
Bellechasse, then cross the L. S. Senghor footbridge

Main events held in the garden

The 'Rendez-vous aux jardins' gardening
event and the 'Jardins, jardin' gardening
and exterior design event: on the first
weekend in June
The European Heritage Days event
(museums and historical sites, normally
closed to the public, open their doors):
the third weekend in September
The International Contemporary Art Fair
(Foire Internationale d'Art Contemporain):
the third week in October

The Librairie du jardin des Tuileries

(A bookshop that specialises in books
on gardening)
Located near the Place de la Concorde,
at the Tuileries Gardens' main gate
Open every day from 10:00 a.m. to 7:00 p.m.

**To ensure that the grounds, plants, and
sculptures are maintained in good condition
and for the purposes of hygiene and security,
it is forbidden to:**

– ride a unicycle or travel on two wheels;
– walk and sit on the lawns;
– pick and damage the plants, including
  through sport activities;
– touch, hold onto, or climb on the sculptures;
– cover the sculptures, walls, furniture,
  and trees with graffiti and tags;
– bring pets (except on the Feuillants
  and Bord-de-l'Eau terraces);
– feed the birds;
– take chairs outside the garden;
– leave an object or bag unattended.

**Security and public-spiritedness are everyone's
concern. This cultural and natural heritage is
fragile, so let's protect it!**

*The reception and surveillance staff are at your
disposal for any further information you may
require.*

PHOTO CREDITS

© 2016. Photo Scala, Florence – courtesy of the Ministero Beni e Att. Culturali: p. 11 • © 2016. The British Library Board/ Scala, Florence: p. 30 • © AGIP / Bridgeman Images: p. 62, p. 64 • © Alinari Archives / CORBIS n°AVQ-A-001169-0004: p. 52 • © Charmet Archives / Bridgeman Images: p. 55 • © Arnaud Chicurel / Hemis / Corbis: p. 16-17 • © Arnaud Madelénat: p. 82-83, p. 88-89 • © Bibliothèque nationale de France: p. 14, p. 18-19, p. 23 on top, p. 29, p. 31 at the bottom • © Bibliothèque Nationale, Paris, France / Bridgeman Images: p. 13 at the bottom • © Château de Versailles, dist. RMN-Grand Palais / Christophe Fouin: p. 42 at the bottom • © Daniel Thierry / Photononstop Agence Photononstop: p. 50-51 • © Dimitri Kessel / The LIFE Premium Collection / Getty Images: p. 63 • © Élise Hardy / RAPHO: p. 71 • © Fotolia / Laufer: p. 65 right • © Fotolia / Renáta Sedmáková: p. 27 • © Hervé Bernard: p. 20 on top, p. 65 at the bottom left, p. 66-67, p. 68 at the bottom, p. 70, p. 73, p. 85, p. 87 on top • © Hulton Archive / Intermittent: p. 57 • © Keystone-France / Gamma-Keystone: p. 61 on top • © Léon et Lévy / Roger-Viollet: p. 56 at the bottom • © Look and Learn / Bridgeman Images: p. 43 on top • © Madrabothair | Dreamstime.com: p. 76-77 • © Maurice-Louis Branger / Roger-Viollet: p. 31 on top • © Musée Carnavalet / Roger-Viollet: p.12 at the bottom • © Musée Condé, Chantilly, France / Bridgeman Images: p. 42 on top • © Musée d'Orsay, dist. RMN-Grand Palais / Patrice Schmidt: p. 53 at the bottom • © Musée de la Ville de Paris, Musée Carnavalet, Paris, France / Bridgeman Images: p. 35 • © Musée du Louvre, dist. RMN-Grand Palais / Thierry Ollivier: p. 44 on top • © Musée du Louvre, dist. RMN-Grand Palais / Antoine Mongodin: p. 22 on top, p. 59-60, p. 75-75, p. 78, p. 79, p. 80, p. 81 on top, p. 87 at the bottom • © Musée du Louvre, dist. RMN-Grand Palais / Christophe Fouin: p. 12 on top, p. 32-33, p. 40-41 • © Musée du Louvre, dist. RMN-Grand Palais / Olivier Ouadah: p. 20 at the bottom • © Musée du Louvre, dist. RMN-Grand Palais / Pierre Philibert: p. 8-9, p. 22 at the bottom, p. 23 bas, p. 43 bas, p. 45 top left, p. 86 • © Musée du Louvre, dist. RMN-Grand Palais / Régine Rosenthal: p. 25-26, p. 45 on top droite, p. 69, p. 72 • © Musée Marmottan Monet, Paris, France / Bridgeman Images: p. 4 • © Philippe Caron / Sygma / Corbis: p. 68 on top • © Philippe Fuzeau : cover and back cover © Photo BnF, Dist. RMN-Grand Palais / image BnF: p. 10 • © Photo by Photo12 / UIG / Getty Images: p. 34 • © Photo RMN-Grand Palais (musée de l'Orangerie) / Gérard Blot / Hervé Lewandowski: p. 13 on top • © Private Collection / Bridgeman Images: p. 53 on top • © PVDE / Bridgeman Images: p. 65 top left • © RMN - Grand Palais (domaine de Compiègne) / Franck Raux: p. 44 at the bottom • © RMN-Grand Palais (Château de Fontainebleau) / Gérard Blot: p. 38 • © RMN-Grand Palais (château de Fontainebleau) / Jean-Pierre Lagiewski: p. 39 • © RMN-Grand Palais (Château de Versailles) / Daniel Arnaudet / Hervé Lewandowski: p. 36-37 • © RMN-Grand Palais (Château de Versailles) / Gérard Blot: p. 21 • © RMN-Grand Palais (musée de la Renaissance, château d'Ecouen) / René-Gabriel Ojéda: p. 15 • © RMN-Grand Palais (musée du Louvre) / René-Gabriel Ojéda: p. 61 at the bottom • © RMN-Grand Palais / Agence Bulloz: p. 28 • © Robert Doisneau / RAPHO: p. 60 • © Robert Holmes / CORBIS: p. 6 • © Sophie Chivet / VU': p. 84 • © Stéphane Ouzonoff / Photononstop: p. 81 at the bottom • © The Art Archive / Gervais Courtellemont / NGS Image Collection: p. 54 • © The National Gallery, Londres, Dist. RMN-Grand Palais / National Gallery Photographic Department: p. 48-49

Cropped pictures : p. 4, p. 29, p. 42, p. 53, p. 56, p. 62

Photoengraving by Quat'Coul, Toulouse.
Printed by PBTisk (Czech Republic) in May 2016.